ALL THAT LIES
BETWEEN US

ESSENTIAL POETS SERIES 153

MARIA MAZZIOTTI GILLAN

ALL THAT LIES

BETWEEN US

GUERNICA

TORONTO — BUFFALO — CHICAGO — LANCASTER (U.K.)

2007

Antonio D'Alfonso, editor
Guernica Editions Inc.
P.O. Box 117, Station P, Toronto (ON), Canada M5S 2S6
2250 Military Road, Tonawanda, N.Y. 14150-6000 U.S.A.

Distributors:
University of Toronto Press Distribution,
5201 Dufferin Street, Toronto (ON), Canada M3H 5T8
Gazelle Book Services, White Cross Mills, High Town,
Lancaster LA1 4XS U.K.
Independent Publishers Group,
814 N. Franklin Street, Chicago, Il. 60610 U.S.A.

First edition.
Printed in Canada.

Legal Deposit – First Quarter
National Library of Canada
Library of Congress Catalog Card Number: 2006940788
Library and Archives Canada Cataloguing in Publication
Gillan, Maria M.
All that lies between us / Maria Mazziotti Gillan.
(Essential poets series ; 153)
ISBN 978-1-55071-261-2
I. Title. II. Series.
PS3557.I375A75 2007   811'.54   C2006-907003-2

Contents

People Who Live Only in Photographs

My mantle is lined with photographs of the dead;
those people who live only in black and white.
Their faces, serious and self-contained, watch
sofas and chairs.

Dennis's great-grandmother and great-grandfather
stand in their Victorian wedding clothes: he, in his
stiff high-necked shirt, black suit; she, in her
high-necked gown, starched and pleated bodice,
plumed hat. They are not smiling, but look
prosperous and poised, a standard photo, circa 1892.

And here is Dennis's father as a young man
in his captain's uniform, a Bing Crosby look-alike.
He is pleased with himself and the world, next
to my father at sixteen in his first posed photograph,
proud and serious in his high-topped shoes,
dark suit and white collar, a formal bouquet
of flowers on the table. It is this photograph
his mother carried until she died, though he left
Italy when he was sixteen and never saw her again.

My grandmothers, whom I never met, stare
out of inexpensive frames. Beside Dennis's
grandmothers, who sit stately in their sterling
oval frames, look poor and worn.

Looking at them, these people I see every day,
I think how little I know to tell a snippet of a story,
a name – nothing else. How little of their past
we can pass on to our own children and grandchildren.
My mother did piecework in a factory for fifty years,
sewing sleeves in coats for a few cents apiece.

I tried to piece together the past of these people
who exist now only in frames by asking questions,
but there is no one left to ask.

I wrote poems about my children as they grew up,
my mother and father, small bits I remembered
about my grandparents. I think now these poems are photos
of a past whose details otherwise no one would know.

Little House on the Prairie

After I found the *Little House on the Prairie*
books in the Riverside branch of the Paterson
Public Library, I read them all, my eyes moving
fast across the page, and then read them all
again, fascinated by the family's journey over mountains,
across plains, admiring the courage
it took to travel that huge emptiness to get
to a place they'd never been,

while I sat in Mr. Landgraff's seventh grade
at PS18 in Paterson; Mr. Landgraff
who was sarcastic, mean, and handsome,
in a white-haired, white-man
kind of way. Mr. Landgraff who preferred
the pretty charming girls. Mr. Landgraff
who thought I was too introverted and shy.
I dreamt my way through seventh grade,
imagining myself in that covered wagon,
though I hadn't left Paterson more than twice,

for in *Little House* I found the bravery
I lacked, reading all evening at home
and walking to school in the morning,
sitting where Mr. Landgraff told me to sit,
crushable as a caterpillar. But after he marked
off my name in his attendance book, I floated
off to Kansas and Nebraska, sure that, like Laura,

I could be brave, that there was a place out there
where I could live a life as extraordinary
and risky as any I read about in books,
far removed from the chalk dust
and quiet despair of seventh grade

with its green black-out shades,
its picture of George Washington,
its scarred and battered desks
that tried to hold me captive.

What Did I Know About Love

I was twelve. What did I know about love,
about how I would love the boy
who lived next door
for being gentle and kind,
for the way he always acted
as if I were breakable and precious;
someone to be guarded and cared for,
though his father was a drunk
who beat him up, and his mother
was skinny with a cigarette always dangling
from the corner of her mouth.

Where did he learn such tenderness?
What un-smashed corner of himself carried
this sweetness? I think of him sometimes,
the first boy I ever loved, the one
who would be the model of every man
I ever fell for, with his golden hair, wide blue
eyes, clear skin, the long delicate fingers
of his hands, think and remember
how we'd walk home together

from PS 18 down the cracked and broken
sidewalks of 19th Street. One night, his family
moved out. "One step ahead of the bill collectors,"
the neighbors said. I did not see him again,
but I remember the way he'd stop a minute
at my house to watch me head toward
our back stoop, and then he'd turn,
face his own house and hesitate,
gathering himself to go inside.

The Mediterranean

At twenty-three, my mother followed my father
to Paterson from San Mauro, that small town
that clung to a mountaintop. From her window
in that southern Italian village, she glimpsed
the Mediterranean, glistening blue.

In the village, they heard stories of storms
that rose from the sea, swallowed fishermen
and boats. As a child, she heard them,
but loved the sea anyway, her own secret
jewel with its incredible light.

In Paterson, inside our tenement, my mother made
the food she'd grown up cooking, filled the house
with the unforgettable aroma of Mediterranean cuisine,
told us stories of San Mauro, the stone house

where she lived, the well where they drew
their water, the stream where they washed their clothes,
the fields built like steps up the sides of the mountain,
but it was the sea she most remembered.

When she spoke of that huge horizon,
sky scrubbed clean by salt air,
sand white as a bleached handkerchief,
we saw the Mediterranean through my mother's eyes,

vivid flowers of Italian summers always with us.

Christmas Story

My mother didn't believe in toys,
felt they were frills we couldn't afford anyway.
I don't remember ever being given a doll
or any other toy. We had paper dolls, one
or two books of them, and games – cards,
dominoes, Monopoly because we could play
these together: my mother wanted us
to be friends, to stay on our front stoop
where she could keep her eye on us,
but Christmas presents in our house were white cotton
underpants, undershirts, socks. She didn't intend
to be cruel. In Italy, by the time she was seven,
she was cooking for the family – all nine
of them – cleaning the house,
tending the chickens and pigs.
Children had to grow up, no time to waste
on toys, but she wanted us to be happy.
Sometimes when she went downtown
to pay five dollars a week on time
for our refrigerator, she'd bring us a box
of imitation M&M's from Kresge's.
They came in a clear plastic box, bright colors
shining through. We'd try to make them last
because, when they were gone, a new box
might not appear for a month or even two.
We used the boxes as couches for our paper
dolls or runways for pretend cars
made of empty spools of thread,
and we'd make up stories, lying
on the floor between the wall
and the bed. I think of my own children,
how I nearly drowned them in presents
at Christmas: GI Joe and Barbie, tanks

and trucks and Legos and blocks, Barbie's
Dream House and Barbie's Convertible,
Barbie's Shore House and Ken,
as though the child that still lives inside me
could fill those Christmas mornings
with more than plain white underwear.

There Was No Pleasing My Mother

Even the things I did well got on her nerves.
Tobias Wolff

My mother found fault with everything
about me, my wild hair, my sloppiness,

my desire to read books, my children
and the way I raised them. "Imagine,"

she said, "letting children run barefoot
in the house. Why they might step

on a needle," despite the fact
that I didn't sew, so it was unlikely

I'd be able to find a needle to step on
even if I wanted to. She even blamed me

for the cat who'd leap off the couch
and hide as soon as he heard her

enter the house. It's not that she didn't
love me and show it in a hundred ways,

but that I was only safe when I was home,
like the day, shortly after I got engaged,

when I was at a girlfriend's house
with five other girls. It started to snow,

and though my girlfriend's house was ten blocks
from my own, my mother called up and said,

"Come home. It's snowing. You're going to lose
your ring." We laughed so hard, my friends and I,

that, as soon as the laughter died down,
we'd start again, and for years they all teased me,

"Come home. It's snowing. You'll lose your ring."
They'd mimic my mother's deeply accented voice,

and I'd laugh too, though part of me didn't
believe I could do anything without her.

Breakfast at IHOP

This morning, I watch the somber man sitting
at a nearby table, book open before him,
two place settings, sit alone. He takes out
his cell phone and dials. I hear his half

of the conversation and try not to look
at him because I see his friend has forgotten
him. His voice stutters as they make another
appointment to meet. He tells the waitress

his friend won't be joining him and orders.
I remember the party I was invited to in sixth
grade, that grade when Judy, my best friend
since we were three, found other girls

to be her friends, outgoing girls, pretty girls,
girls who knew how to talk and laugh
with boys the way she did. I ran home
after school on the day of the party.

I left Judy at her house with Diane and Camille.
"I'll wait for you," I said.
I looked out the front window and waited
with my present wrapped in inexpensive paper,

but they never picked me up like they promised.
In that man's face, I see the same shame I felt
that day, to have been forgotten, left behind,
to be so unimportant even your friends

don't remember you.

Vestal, New York

I want to write a poem to celebrate

my father's arms, bulging and straining while he carries
the wooden box of purple grapes down the crumbling,

uneven cement steps into the cellar of the old house
on 19th Street. The cellar, whitewashed by my mother,

grows darker as my father lumbers past the big coal
furnace and into the windowless wine room

at the back where he will feed the grapes,
ripe and perfect and smelling of earth,

into the wine press. The grape smell changes
as they are crushed and drawn out into fat

wooden barrels, and for weeks the cellar
will be full to the brim with the sweet smell

of grapes fermenting into wine, a smell I recognize
even forty years later each time I uncork a bottle,

an aroma that brings back my father
and his friends gathering under Zio Gianni's

grape arbor to play briscole through long July
nights, small glasses before them, peach slices

gleaming like amber in the ruby wine.

Superman

Superman was my brother's hero: Clark Kent with his
horn-rimmed glasses, just like my brother's, transformed
into someone who could leap tall buildings
in a single bound, and Lois Lane who loved him.

This was 1950s TV and the girl was always
the foil for the hero, the one who helped
but never took center stage. I never wanted
to be like that. I wanted to be the one

who made things happen, though there were no
super girls in 1950. This was right after the war,
and when the men came home, they wanted
their jobs back, wanted their women in aprons

to put their dinners on the table as soon
as they walked in the door. I'd seen
my mother in her homemade apron
struggling to cook everything from scratch,

cooking and canning and cleaning.
This didn't appeal to me, though
I knew I would marry. I was supposed
to marry. Everyone did. But when I graduated

from high school I knew what I didn't want:
to be married and pregnant like some
of my girlfriends, right before they graduated,
or right after. I didn't want to go

to William Paterson College as my mother wished,
to be a kindergarten teacher so I could be at home
when my children had finished their days at school.
"I want to go to college, be a writer,"

I announced, not listening when my accountant cousin
said this was the most impractical ambition he'd ever
heard of. "I want to be a writer," knowing
that I would never play Lois Lane to a Superman.

Tenacious as a bulldog, I kept trying, even
though I knew my cousin was right. It was
an impractical ambition, but one I couldn't trade
for any other, since words were the way

I could leap tall buildings in a single bound.

I Am Thinking of the Dress

I am thinking of the dress I wore
to my senior prom, pale blue chiffon

with a nipped-in waist and a swirly skirt
that cost more money than my mother

could afford but bought for me
anyway, even though pale blue

is not a good color for a dark-skinned girl,
but rather for the girl I wished I could be.

I wore that dress with high heels and nylons,
garter belt and a lace bra. I went to the prom

with Jimmy, the boy I dated senior year,
a boy I didn't love and who didn't love me.

The prom was at the North Jersey Country Club,
and after dinner, the couples scattered

out to the grounds, couples draped
on the lounge chairs around the pool. Lois

and Bill, our best friends, went into the woods.
When they came back Lois's dress was stained

and crumpled and they acted proud of themselves.
Jimmy and I walked around the pool. He held

my hand. We sat on a bench and he kissed me
and kissed me and nothing happened – no spark

at all. I think of him now, poor Jimmy,
trying so hard to make people think

he was straight, like me sitting on that stone
bench in my beautiful blue dress

trying to make people believe
I could get a handsome date.

My Father's Fig Trees
in Hawthorne, New Jersey

Each winter, my father wrapped his fig trees
in burlap and buried them; each spring

he lifted them out of the earth and unwrapped
them. How they turned toward the sun

in their flowering, grew hundreds of fat purple
fruit that my father picked each day,

washing them off and presenting them to me
as though they were diamonds or pearls.

I paid people to empty my parents' house
of fifty years of accumulation, to sell

their things to the first bidder. I hid
from the task of packing and sorting,

each item a reminder. This one last thing
I could have done in their honor

was too much, the guilt and shame
twin scarves I wear for the place that broke

inside me when I couldn't manage
and hid in my bed for weeks.

I pass my parents' house and want
to stop, to walk into the small backyard

to see if the fig trees are still there.
I could not manage to find someone

to dig up the trees, replant them at my house
and, instead, left them for people

who do not know how much of that Italian
mountain village my father left

when he was sixteen was in that rich fruit,
the earthy sweetness of it, the way my father

did not eat the figs himself, but always
saved them for me.

My Sister and Frank Sinatra

My cousin says, "You're the last person alive
from my childhood," and we both nearly begin

to cry, two ladies heading out for lunch
in my cousin's sleek new convertible. Before

she starts the car she hands me
an old photograph. At the forefront

my sister looks out at the camera.
In the photo she is twenty-five,

just married. I had forgotten
how exquisitely beautiful she was as a girl,

her full sensuous lips, her large chocolate brown
eyes, the sweetheart curve of her Elizabeth

Taylor face, her Marilyn Monroe body.
Waves of energy came off her. By the time

she died at sixty-two, crippled in a wheelchair,
she struggled against the narrowing

frame of her life, retreated gradually
away from us, ashamed of her twisted

and crooked hands, her feet
so distorted that she had to wear ugly shoes

specially made for her. When she was a girl,
legs slender, size-five feet beautifully formed,

she loved to dance in high heels,
twirling around the dance floor doing the rhumba

and the jitterbug. We'd listen to Sinatra when we'd ride
around in my cousin's used car, an old black Ford:

my sister, her friend Florence, and my cousin,
riding out of constricted Paterson streets

to the wider country lanes of Bergen County.
We thought it would be as easy as that,

our lives utterly changed if we found the man
we longed for, the love Sinatra made us sure

was real. We were the Happily Ever After Girls,
believed in that myth like we believed nothing else.

I hold my sister's picture in my hand, feel the
weight of that past, those 1950s girls, the way

happiness is water you can't hold in your hands.
We didn't know then that, like our mothers,

those women we vowed we'd never be,
we'd end up making do with whatever

presented itself before us.

Sunday Dinners at My Mother's House

After I was grown up and had a house
and a family of my own, my mother cooked
and served dinner for all of us, her children
and grandchildren, at least sixteen people
each Sunday in her basement kitchen.
My mother was an artist of food,
and we gathered around three tables lined up,
end to end, macaroni and meatballs, braciola,
salad and roasted chicken, potatoes and stuffed
artichokes, fruit and nuts with their own silvery
nutcrackers, apple pies and turnovers,
espresso and anisette.

Every Sunday the courses emerged from that kitchen
and arrived at the table as if by magic: my mother,
moving like a dervish between the kitchen
and the finished room that was our cellar
dining room in that tiny house, that wouldn't hold
all of us in the dining room upstairs. The upstairs
kitchen, clean and untouched, was almost never used,
except to serve coffee to guests we didn't know well,
while the family and friends all gathered in the cellar
to eat and talk politics and baseball: the cousins,
whispering and giggling at the end table,
and the rest of us as excited and loud as a convention
of beer salesmen, except for my brother, the doctor,
always soft-spoken. My father and I,
the political radicals, the loudest of all
in our convictions.

My father, at ninety-two, asked me to take him
in his wheelchair to march on Washington.
"The people are asleep," he said.
"We have to try to wake them up."
My mother didn't care about politics at all;
she only cared about us, about keeping us
all close to her and together.
"When you have trouble," she said,
"only your family will help you,"
and we all came back to be near her,
back to that blue-collar town where she lived,
my sister's house across the street from mine,
my brother's on top of the hill,
my mother's not five minutes away.
I'd see her smiling, happy that we were all
together, willing to cook for all of us, week
after week, to make sure we'd stay that way.

In my mother's kitchen, there were always
stories and laughter, arguments and excitement.
When I was nineteen I went to a friend's house
for dinner. It was the first time I sat at a table
where no one spoke, no stories or conversation
or laughter, only pass the potatoes please,
the mother sitting stiff as a stick at one end
of the table, the father at the other, his mouth
a staple in his somber face. I was glad to go home.

Now it is ten years since my mother died,
four since my father's death, two since my sister's.
My son and his family are in North Carolina;
my daughter in Cambridge; my brother's son in Chicago.
I remember my father saying when my son moved
away, not a year after my mother was dead,
"Without your mother the chain is broken."

28

My Father Always Drove

My father always drove. My mother sat
in the passenger seat giving directions,
advising him when to turn or when to slow
down, though it's hard to imagine him driving
any slower. His top speed was ten miles an hour,
even in that bright red Ford he bought secondhand,

the one my mother was so upset about
after his old blue Chevy collapsed.
He had to pay someone to take it away.
He went off with one of his friends
to look at used cars and drove into our

driveway in that bright red Ford.
My mother thought the car called
attention to itself, and never climbed
into that car without telling my father
what she thought of it. But it took her

where she had to go: grocery shopping,
doctor's office, grandchildren-sitting
on Friday nights. It took my father
to visit his friends where he played cards
and talked politics. My father always drove.

All her kindergarten year, while I taught
college, he took my daughter to school
and picked her up, taught her to play cards
with him; her face, concentrated and serious,

above the Queen of Hearts and Jacks.
My father drove that red car
until he was eighty-six. Everyone
in town knew him, the old guy
who drove five miles an hour

through the center of town,
always ready to bring us,
his children and grandchildren,
a gift, a paper sack of fresh figs

from his trees, tomatoes from the garden,
chocolate candies for the children, silver dollars
he'd saved, lottery tickets he hoped would win
us a million. Even our cat knew him.

The cat would sit on the front porch watching.
When my father would turn the corner
onto Oak Place, the cat would leap off
the porch and race down the street
toward him, following the car to the house

and following my father inside. My father arrived,
carrying a foil-wrapped package of liver or fish,
happy to give gifts, even to this cat,
who purred for him.

Spike-Heels

In the 1950s, I wore spike-heels.
They were very high, but I was thin then,

didn't wobble. I walked through hours
at my job, my high heels twinkly

as Dorothy's red slippers with pointy toes,
heels in every possible color, sling-backs

and pumps, the clickety-clack of them
on pavement making me feel

as sophisticated as Marilyn Monroe. Older now,
my heels have gone lower and lower,
reduced to sandals with Velcro straps to hold
my triple E-feet. I still watch women

striding in their spike-heels, and wish
for one minute that I could go back
to the days when I could walk

with such grace, look with longing
at this marker of beauty, as though

I were still sixteen and not this woman
I've become, pounding through life

on confident feet.

Trying to Get You to Love Me

When we were young, I made lists of ways
to get you to love me. I'd try to make you

jealous by talking about the places I'd gone,
though I didn't mention the name

of the other man I was dating. Your friend Paul,
whom I hated because he was obnoxious

and seemed to control you, told you
that going out on Saturday night was

cliché. So you'd take me out on Friday
or Sunday, which worked out well for me

because I went out with Frank on Tuesday
and Saturday. Frank squired me to expensive

restaurants in New Jersey and to dinner theater
and took me on long drives into New York State

where we'd eat at an expensive restaurant
and drive back home. He told me

how he made a million dollars by buying
a farm from a farmer one afternoon

and selling it to someone else an hour
later for forty times the amount

he'd paid, and about a housing development
he was building in Mahwah. He took me

through the model home, told me
he'd save sixty-five dollars a house

because he'd put in a counter rather than
a vanity with shelves and doors.

You took me to New York City to hear
folk singers like Pete Seeger, and to the Cloisters,

the Botanical Gardens and the Bronx Zoo.
Once on the way home from a drive

into New York State, Frank stopped the car
at a lookout and began to kiss me

and to try to take my blouse off. I told him
I couldn't, that I had to go home. When you

and I parked at Palisades Park on the edge
of the cliffs with the New York view,

I would have done anything you asked.
I thought you were beautiful, the prototype

of every man I'd ever loved with your blond
hair, blue eyes, high cheekbones and light skin,

the opposite of all the Italian boys I knew.
But I didn't know whether you loved me

or thought me beautiful. I looked at *Seventeen*
magazine and *Mademoiselle*, tried to read

all the articles about how to get a man, but still
I was never sure. One day I said I'd been

to Trader Vic's in New York City (with Frank,
of course, but I didn't say that), and you started

shouting at me. "I don't know what you're doing,"
you said. "Do you love me, or not?" I tried to explain,

to say that I didn't know what you felt,
that you never asked me to go steady,

never talked about anything more
than our next date. By the end of the evening,

we were engaged. I told Frank the next day
that I couldn't see him anymore. He was furious

and, for two years, he refused to talk to my friend
who introduced us. I didn't care. Though I felt

a little guilty, mostly I could see the lives ahead
of us in Technicolor, the wedding cake,

the honeymoon, the house and children,
and you, the man I loved and married.

Housework and Buicks with Fins

When we were first married, Dennis bought a
1957 Buick, pale blue and white, with huge fins

to replace the dilapidated brown Pontiac
he used to drive. I owned a Sapphire blue

Volkswagen, with a sun roof, which was easy
to maneuver in and out of spaces.

It was the only car I'd ever driven.
When I looked at Dennis's Buick, I couldn't

imagine how I'd steer that yacht of a car down
the crowded streets of Hawthorne and Paterson.

One day my car was being repaired and I had
to take Dennis's car to run an errand,

but, when I got to the store and tried to
parallel park, I couldn't manage and had to go

back home. I pulled into the driveway
of the small Cape Cod house we bought before

we were married, the house that *I* bought
because I had saved enough money for a down-

payment. My sister and mother and I had
scrubbed the filthy floors in that house

with Brillo because it was the only way
to get it clean, and we painted it and threw out

the junk the former owners left behind. I
realize now that Dennis didn't help at all,

though I don't know why it didn't occur to me
then, nor did I realize that I was setting up

a pattern for the way things would be, married
to my 1950s husband who expected me to be

the 1950s wife he thought he'd married, both of us
babied by our mothers, mine who poured my

milk and buttered my toast until the day I left,
and his mother who served all his meals

to him in the dining room so that he had never
cleaned a pan or cooked a meal for himself.

We had a wild first six months of marriage. I was
waiting for him to serve me, he was waiting for

me to serve him, until finally I realized what I
should have known before the wedding march

and white gown, should have known when
I was on my hands and knees scrubbing

that floor – if anything was going to get done,
I'd have to do it myself, all except driving

that huge Buick. That I left to him.

Driving into Our New Lives

Years ago, driving across the mountains
in West Virginia, both of us are so young
we don't know anything. We are twenty-eight
years old, our children sleeping in the back seat.
With your fresh Ph.D. in your suitcase, we head out
toward Kansas City. We've never been anywhere.
We decide to go the long way around
instead of driving due west.

Years ago, driving across mountains, your
hand resting on my knee, the radio playing the folk
music we love, Pete Seeger, Joan Baez, or you
singing songs to keep the children entertained.
How could we know what is to come?

We are young. We think we'll be healthy
and strong forever. We are certain we are invincible
because we love each other, because our children
are smart and beautiful, because we are heading

to a new place, because the stars
in the coal-black West Virginia sky are so thick,
they could be chunks of ice.
How could we know what is to come?

Nighties

At my bridal shower, someone gave me
a pink see-through nightgown and pink satin
slippers with slender heels and feathers.
The gown had feathers on it too.

I've always hated my legs and even then,
when I was still thin and in good shape,
I didn't want to wear that nightgown
or slippers, didn't want to parade

in front of you like some pin-up.
But I wore them anyway, all those negligées
I got as shower presents, sleazy nylon
I didn't know was tacky. When I wore

shorty nightgowns, I'd leap into bed
not wanting you to notice how
the nightgown revealed what I thought
my biggest flaw. In all the young years

of our marriage, I wore a different nightgown
every night, not that it ever stayed on for long,
and afterwards I'd pull it back on, not wanting
our children to find me naked in our bed.

I felt so sophisticated in those nightgowns,
like the ones Doris Day wore in movies.
Only years later, when my daughter buys me
a nightgown made of soft and smooth blue silk,

do I realize that the first ones I owned
were cheap imitations of this, the one
I hold now to my cheek, grateful
to have been once what I was.

How lucky I am to have loved you
in nylon, silk, my own incredible skin.

In the Movies No One Ever Ages

I wish I could say the same for me,
but that's what's so wonderful about the movies.
The people on the screen remain as they were,
yet for me, when I look back at our lives,
you too are caught in freeze-frame, light
coming off you, the planes of your handsome
face, your perfect, muscular body.
Do you remember walking through
the New York Botanical Gardens?
You, your mind filled with facts
like an encyclopedia, your photographic
memory, told me all about the flowers
and birds and the trees inside the towering
greenhouses. We walked and kissed behind
the exuberant vegetation of the African rainforest,
tropical birds skimming the air above our heads.

Do you remember the concert
at Columbia too and how exciting
it was to hear Pete Seeger sing in person?
We walked together across that moonlit campus.
These moments are what I hold now when
I see you struggling to win against a disease
that has robbed you of almost everything.
Each day is one less thing you can do,
though you can still hold my hand,
put your frail arms around me.

Who Knew How Lonely
the Truth Can Be

When I was still timid and shy I hated
people who told the truth, bluntly,

blurting out that you had a big nose
or that your shampoo smelled cheap. Then

I studied Keats and his claim that poetry
is truth and beauty and I had no idea

what he was talking about until I was forty
years old and saw how truth in a poem

makes the hair on the back of my neck rise.
Now, when I am the one blurting out truths that

often leave people staring, when I say at my
department meeting the very thing that others won't,

how alone I become as I speak, a space
cleared around me as though I have

the plague. That loneliness I can stand. The other
loneliness, the truth we can barely admit to ourselves

at three a.m. when we're lying in bed unable
to sleep, that truth, the one too ugly to admit,

how we want to climb to the top of a tower
and shake off all the arms that need

our comfort and the way we need
to be selfish, to climb into that tower

and not let down our hair, to be
for at least a little while

only for ourselves,
selfish and quiet and alone.

I Wish I Knew How to Tell You

My fear the other night, the night
when we went out to dinner
and I hauled you in your collapsible
wheelchair to the restaurant
where we had dinner so many times
when you could still walk

you so frail looking and nervous
because your arms flap around
like angry birds, and you knock
things off the table,
sure that people are looking at you.
"It's getting worse," you say. *"I'm scared."*
I hear your words and think

how caught we are in our own skins,
how hard it is to feel what someone else
feels. I think I'm sympathetic. I think I'm kind.
I want to believe that,
but, when we get home, I get violently sick

from food poisoning, shivering so badly
I can't keep my hands still, my teeth chattering.
Finally, after heaving for an hour,
I wrap myself in quilts and get into bed,
this physical assault making my arthritis
flare up so I can't bend my knee

or put my feet on the floor, or move my back
or my hand without pain, and I say to you
who hover around me, "Please leave the door open."
I don't say, "I'm afraid, I don't want to be alone,"
but that's what I mean, and for the first time I,

who am always on the road, my sturdy body
taking me everywhere like a dependable car,
really understand what you feel when you come
to me in your electric wheelchair, the *scrich scrich*
of its wheels on the carpet, your hands trembling,
your face pale and perspiring, your eyes avoiding mine.
"I'm afraid," you say. "Hold my hand."

What a Liar I Am

I have been lying for a long time now,
the sicker you get the more I lie
to myself most of all. I cannot say
how angry I am that this illness
is another person in our house, so lies
are the only way to get through each day.

How hard it is to admit that I am often
impatient and raging and that anger
is a pit I can never swallow, that love,
even mine for you who have been with me
forty years, cannot dissolve the hank
of loneliness that has become lodged

in my throat, the irritating squeaking
of your electric wheelchair, the way
I want to run from the putrid smell
of medicines rising from your skin,
the way I lie and lie so you won't know

how heavy this illness feels. How long
it has been going on, sixteen years now.
Your feet, dragging along the carpet
on days you can still walk,
are like a fingernail on a blackboard.
"This is all too much for you," you say,
and I reassure you, "No, not for you,

nothing is too much for you."
"I am a burden," you say,
and "No, no," I say. "Not a burden."

The face I see in my mirror is not one
I want to see. O love, I could not
have imagined it would come to this,
when I can only live by lying to myself
and you, you with your begging eyes,
your reedy voice, a clanging bell that calls me,
you whom I love but cannot carry.

On an Outing to Cold Spring

In the photograph my arm is around your waist,
my head leans against your shoulder, the sun washes
your hair in light. In the background a cardboard
cut-out of a beautiful Victorian lady in a straw hat
watches us, a scowl on her face.
We do not see her. The picture captures
the frozen look of the muscles of your face,
though you still look handsome. The disease
has only just begun to take hold. We are
on an outing to Cold Spring Harbor.
You have no trouble walking. I convince myself
this is as bad as it will be.
The woman behind us knows more than I do.

Yesterday, I go to the lawyer who advises me
to get a bed and board divorce or, she says,
"You will be impoverished." I am so nervous
when she speaks to me that I have to
keep asking her to repeat what she is saying
so I can write it down. "Look," she says, "he
isn't going to get better, only worse.
You have to try to protect yourself." Later,
I sit with you, explain what she advised,
try to keep my voice from splitting apart
and you say, "I want you to be safe.
A divorce," you say, and your hands shake.
"Only a bed and board divorce –
not a real divorce," I say.

In the lawyer's office, her conference room with its exposed
brick walls, her framed Van Gogh posters,
her handmade antique quilt hanging on the walls,
she asks what your condition is now. I explain.
She says, "The law allows you to do this."

In our family room, you sit next to me
in your wheelchair. You reach out
to touch my face. I hold you and stare
over your shoulders at this picture
of us, standing in that garden, oblivious
to how much it is possible to lose,
and I know the subtext in this script,
that today we are admitting
that you are racing downhill
like an out-of-control sled,
and nothing I can do will stop you.

Selective Memory

Our daughter tells me I practice selective
memory, that I erase the parts of the past
I don't like or don't want to know.
I denied it, but then I thought maybe
she was right after all, that maybe I need
to soften the sharp edges of memory, as though
I were working colored chalk over a painting.

So it must have been selective memory
that I was practicing when I let myself
forget that I've always loved my husband
more than he loved me, that fact I forced
myself to forget as he grew ill and we grew
together over the years, moments glittering
like gold in rock, the way those remembered
glimpses of a beloved face, or the feel
of a hand or words spoken softly stay
with us and run like a vein through the lives
of couples like us, long married and happy
together, our lives growing to fit us
like another skin,

and it must be selective memory that makes me
remember the explosion of love between us and not
the anger with which we fought when we were
young and before you got sick.

One night, sitting in our bed, I am raving
and furious that my friend who cried
at his wife's funeral two months ago
is already going dancing each night.
I say, "He'll probably be married within six months,"
and you say, "If something happened to you I

would remarry, why not?" And your words sting worse
than if you had stabbed me, who wanted – no,
expected – to hear that you wouldn't want anyone
but me, even if you were lying, the kind
of lie we all tell to protect those we love,
and "I can't believe you," I say,
and you say, "Why not? Why not?"
And I think that our daughter is right,
that I practice selective memory. I am angry
thinking of you, like my friend spending
his wife's money on someone else,
and I wish you had lied to me
as I lie to you so often
to protect you.

For a moment I see you in your electric
wheelchair dancing around the room
with another woman, passing my money
on to her instead of our children
and grandchildren. I cannot believe
how furious I am.

For a few days I don't let my pity
for you touch my heart, and then
we are watching the debates together:
you in your wheelchair and me
on the sofa. I watch you, your face
twitching and moving, your neck twisting,
your arms jerking, and I remember
how much I love you, and would,
even if you married someone else,
even if I had to return from my grave
to haunt you, even then, I can't help
the tenderness I still feel
when I look at you.

Your Voice on the Phone Wobbles

Your voice on the phone wobbles and sounds tight
as one of the strings of your guitar,

the one you used to play when you could
still sing. From my motel room, I try

to smooth away your shaking, as I would
if I were at home with you, smoothing

my hand across your shoulders until the muscles
unknot. "Where are you?" I ask,
and you say you're upstairs at your

computer. I can tell you are frantic
because the message you're trying to send

to the Computer Help Line keeps
getting erased. Your hands no longer work

the way you want them to. I am afraid
you will fall downstairs in your distraction,

the woman who helps you already gone.
Last week you insisted you could walk.

It was only ten in the morning, and you said
you could always walk until at least 11:30.

I drove you to the drugstore. We walked inside.
I got a cart for you to lean on,

but you didn't want it. I left you standing
in an aisle looking for shaving lotion.

I was looking at the rows of cough
medicine and cold remedies when I heard

a crash. I rushed into the next aisle
and found you struggling to get up

from the floor. I helped you up,
tried to talk you into leaning

on the cart. You refused. Two minutes later,
you fell again, the way you do, as though

you were a felled tree. I pretended
people weren't staring at us. Tonight

with your voice so ragged, I try to talk
you into going downstairs to your chair,

try to get you to give up on the computer
and read a book. I feel like your

mother, scolding, prodding. I don't know
the exact day or year when things changed

like this between us. They say in each
relationship the person who loves the most

gives all the power to the one who doesn't
love as much. I was besotted with you,

bent myself to your will. Maybe it was this
illness, your need of me suddenly greater

than mine for you, that made me seem
more valuable, more cherished,

so I can tell that two days since
I left home you need me back, the way

you never would have needed me then.

On Thanksgiving This Year

Two days before Thanksgiving I take you
to a Parkinson's Research Center
where the doctor says you are over-
medicated and cuts back on medicine
by thirty percent. You start the regimen
the next day and, by Thanksgiving,
you are having so much trouble moving,
Jennifer and I take you across the street
in your collapsible wheelchair and lift
you out of it and onto my niece's sofa.
When we help you to the table, I watch
you turning into an old man on some
pill that works the opposite of the fountain
of youth, your head bends forward
so your chin touches your chest
and you are incomprehensible
when you try to speak.
Your fork falls from your hand
when you try to lift it. I watch you struggle,
ask in a whisper if I can help you.
"No," you say, "no, I need to go home."
We lift you into the wheelchair
and your body looks like the body
of a ninety-year-old man,
though you are only sixty-five.
At home again, you are unable
to eat your dinner. You have an accident.
Jennifer and I struggle to get your wet
clothes off and put on clean clothes,
and that happens three times,
and by the third time I am about to cry.
You say, "Shoot me. Please shoot me."
"Don't worry," I say.

Don't worry, it will be okay."
And then Jennifer takes over
and says, "Go sit down for a minute."
She changes you again.
You cry. Finally, we put you to bed
with a book, prop the book up for you
because your hands won't hold it. In the middle
of the night, I, who sleep like the dead, don't
hear you call, and Jennifer gets up to help
you out of bed to use the urinal. In the morning,
I finally reach the neurologist who says,
"That's called a crash. They used
to put PD patients in the hospital
when they cut back these drugs."
He says to put you back on the medicine
and we do. Gradually you come back
to yourself, and though it's not good,
you're not totally paralyzed. But the image
of you incontinent, frozen, is the elephant
in the room with us, the one I try to ignore,
though I know it's there. "Have you
taken care of the money?" you ask.
"You know – don't you? – that I'm going to be
like that by the end of next year."

I Never Tell People

I never tell people that I almost left you
twenty years ago, don't tell them how your rage

terrified me when I watched you pick up
the sugar bowl and hurl it at the wall,

don't tell them about the summer we painted
the bedrooms and you screamed and screamed

out the open windows until I yelled back
and the neighbors came out to water their lawns

so they could hear, don't tell them about
the time you were so angry at me

that we fought on the stairs and you punched
me and I punched back. I shouted, "I want

a divorce," and you went totally still
and said, "No, no, I won't give you one,"

and then you said, "See. I knew you never
loved me." I took the keys and drove around

Bergen County for hours. When I came back
it was getting dark and we tiptoed

around each other, afraid of the chasm
that had opened between us. In our bed

that night, after the children fell asleep,
you got me back the way you always did,

sex, the way you soothed my hurt feelings,
the bruises on my arms where you punched me,

the way you whistled in the shower after
the latest argument had lost the power

to harm. I never tell anyone how I blamed
myself for the broken places inside you.

I tried to stay out of the way when you slapped
your own face or banged your head on the wall

for losing a pencil or a notebook or to escape
your father's voice inside you listing all your flaws.

So how then did I come to this place where
I knew I wasn't to blame, that I had to save

what I needed for myself, to keep your fists
from smashing what I was? After all

the arguments, screaming, I stopped feeling
so frightened of your fury. I never tell

anyone that twenty years ago I almost left
you, the two of us caught in the tornado

of your flailing arms, flailing like the way
they move uncontrollably now with your disease,

and found instead this quiet place where you,
the man I hated and loved, are the boat

I rock in each night, almost forgetting
those turbulent years when the sadness

you carried like a rotten tooth in your mouth,
the empty places I could never fill,

nearly broke us.

Do You Know What It Is I Feel?

By evening now, often you can't walk, your thin
frame falling into your electric wheelchair,
the *knuck knuck* of its wheels on the hardwood
floors, the bang and clatter of it hitting
the French doors or the refrigerator,
or scraping along the mahogany furniture
your mother left us.

You finally arrive next to the sofa where
I am curled under the Victorian velvet throw
our daughter gave me. Your chair pulled up
close to the sofa arm, you reach out
for my hand and hold it while we watch
a movie together, my eyes sliding sideways
and looking at you. It's too difficult

to confront you head on, your body growing
thinner with each day, your neck suddenly
too weak to hold up your head. I remember
you when we were young, look at the picture
on the shelf behind us, of you
on the camping trip we took to Swartswood Lake,
you holding the flap of the tent open

for our two-year-old daughter with her blond
ringlets and violet eyes. You look so beautiful
in the dappled light, your shoulders wide
and muscular, your narrow waist, the muscles
of your legs sharply defined against your jeans.
I'd look at you, and my breath

would catch in my throat. Now, when
I look at you, pity is a knife that
cuts me through. The trips I thought we'd take,
the places we'd see together, the old age
I'd imagined has vanished and instead I have,
these few hours when I hold your hand

and don't dare look at you too closely
for fear I will have to know how angry I am
that you have left me when I still have need.

What I Remember

Hot Ovaltine in the 17th Street kitchen
with its scrubbed linoleum and steaming farina.
The coal stove spilled its heat over my back;
the loose windows patterned with ice,
my mother serving us, my mother who rarely
said, "I love you," but showed it
with each stirring
of her cooking pots and spoons.

My father cracked eggs into a thick-sided cup
and stirred them with sugar, making
a ceremony out of handing me the eggs
that were supposed to keep me, his skinny,
weak-chested daughter, from getting sick again.

That kitchen, the soft light of the etched-glass fixture,
the oil cloth-covered table, is that place
I return to when the thought of you
is suddenly too much for me to carry,
this suitcase full of fear, when all my running,
the readings and workshops and lectures and friends
won't allow me to forget.

If I don't think about it, maybe I can
get you back the way you were and not
the shaking voice you have become,
who tells me on the phone last night,
"It's getting worse. Soon I won't be able
to move at all and then what will happen?"
Though I soothe you, my shame is
that I am not with you when you hallucinate
the tie of your robe is a snake or the socks
you left on the floor are mice.

I would take us both back
to the 17th Street kitchen, pull you
into my memory of that place so filled
with soft light and arms that held me.
My father could stir an egg for you
in a cup. My mother break off a piece
of hot bread for you; spread butter on it
from the Lakeview Dairy crock the milkman
delivered. My sister and brother could help
us bake sugar cookies. We could play Monopoly.
We could leave all our grief in a sack by the door.

I Walk Through the Rooms of Memory

I walk through the rooms of memory, counting
my dead. First, my mother with her quick laugh
and her energy and her earthy humor, old wise
woman, who leaves a hole in the center

of my days larger than Times Square;
then, my father with his love of company
and his open heart and his radical politics.
And, finally, my sister who always knew

the quickest way to get something done,
all of them lost to me now. All the rooms
of memory are full of dust, and words
spoken years ago in anger or sorrow festoon

the windows. The voices, that is what remains,
their voices bring them back to me. I see
my mother serving me espresso and cake
at her kitchen table, the one in the basement,

metal with plastic-covered metal chairs,
my mother saying, "I don't have anything
to give you to eat," and then opening the door
of the old Kelvinator and producing pasta

and fagoli or chicken and fish, meatballs
and homemade bread, my mother who never cried
or said, "I love you," but showed it
in everything she did, and my father

sitting at ninety-two in his brown recliner
from Medicare, his shrinking body
overshadowed by the chair meant for someone
so much bigger than he. And Laura, I remember

you as we were when we were girls, you
with your size thirty-six D breasts that men
always wanted to touch and your hourglass
figure and your slender legs and beautiful

size-five feet, you with your big smile

and your perfect teeth, you in your Fire-and-Ice
lipstick, how you loved to dance, how I
loved to watch you move with such unselfconscious
grace and, years later, I see you sitting in the hospital

bed in your den when you got too sick
to leave the house. I am holding your hand,
the bones so twisted by rheumatoid arthritis
that you can't hold a pencil. And your feet,

those feet I remember in their black
high-heeled pumps, those feet now so crippled
the bones poke through the skin. Sometimes
I imagine we are all together again, all of us

as we were so often for those noisy Sunday
dinners: my mother serving course after course
of steaming food; all of us with no idea yet
of how much we have to lose.

Nothing Can Bring Back the Dead

I know, but this morning, driving to the university
with my side view mirror improperly adjusted
so I nearly ran into a shiny red Honda
when I was trying to switch lanes, I think

of my mother, dead now twelve years.
I am driving and talking to her, as
though she were in the car with me
as she was when I was a young mother

and I'd pick her up to take her grocery shopping.
And she'd get into my bright blue VW bug,
and she'd be all neat and shiny, clean
as a polished button. She'd hold her handbag,

imitation leather in beige or black with a small
handle and a little clip to hold it closed,
and start right in complaining about my dirty car.
She'd curse in Italian under her breath

as she picked up scraps of paper,
candy wrappers, the assorted refuse of my life
and placed my garbage in a plastic bag
she'd carried to the car for that purpose.

Even as she cleaned up, wrapping the seat belt
around her like a scarf because she couldn't manage
the buckle, she'd tell me how to drive,
"Slow down, watch out for that car, close

the window, there's a draft in this car" –
even when it was a hundred degrees outside.
Then she'd unsnap her purse, that little click
I can still hear in my head, and she'd take out

a hard candy and give it to me. It was always
like that between us. My mother, who could
make me furious, was the one I came to
for comfort, the one who provided whatever

I needed, so today I am driving and talking
to her. I can feel her presence, as though
I were back in her kitchen, sitting
at her round kitchen table, the place

I came to more and more as I grew
older and my children grew. The older she got,
the more people came to her for her wisdom
and earthy humor, her straight talk, her energy,
her ability to laugh, all of us, leaning

on her, my mother who wasn't even
five feet tall, so that at her funeral,
we all sobbed out loud, daughters, sons,
grandchildren, daughters-in-law, sons-in-law,

this Greek chorus of sobbing because how could
someone so strong and alive have vanished?
When I was thirty, I screamed at her
and threw her out of my house for criticizing

my domestic abilities. I fought with her
over everything until, one day, she changed
and I changed, and she became the one
place in the world where I could be safe,

sitting at her table, sipping espresso and talking.
In this car now, I remember the times
she touched my face, "Oh Tesoro," she used to say,
calling me her treasure, and I reach out
for her now, "Tesoro," I say, and

touch her cheek with my hand.

What I Can't Face
About Someone I Love

That my son loves me but would prefer
not to see me too much. Every Sunday night,

when I call him in North Carolina where
he lives with his wife and two children,

I can hear the heaviness in his voice,
his "Hello" tempered with impatience,

our conversation stiff and stilted, though
I always think I can talk to a stone.

Strangers in buses and trains tell me their life
histories, acquaintances tell me about their affairs

and shattered marriages, show me the secret
undersides of their lives. My graduate students vie

for my attention. They want to sit next to me
and carry my bags and fetch my lunch,

but my son can't wait to get off the phone
with me. I ask him how the kids are

or specific questions about school, ask about

his wife, his job. He answers with one or two
words; "They're fine," or "Okay," or "The same."

My son is a lawyer; he was always brilliant
with language, at least written language,

and he can read a three-hundred page book
in an hour and remember every detail,

but with me he turns mute as a stump.
If I ask for help with some legal problem,

he will give it, but I do not hear in his voice
the lilt I hear in my daughter's voice

when I call her. Instead I hear reluctance,
as though his attention were focused

on some truly fascinating person
and he can't wait to get off the phone.

I tell stories that I hope will amuse him,

but finally, after struggling and finding no response,
I can't wait to hang up. When I can't stand it anymore

I say, "Well, John, have a good week.
Give everyone a hug for me." I know my son

has divorced me, somewhere deep inside
himself in a place he doesn't look at.

I am too much for him, too loud, too dramatic,
too frantic, too emotional. I laugh too much.

I wear him out in a minute and a half. If he never
saw me again he wouldn't miss me and this is what

I can't face about someone I love.

Is This the Way It Is
Between Mothers and Sons?

Is this the way it is with mothers and sons,
this distance that opens between us like a
canyon I can never bridge? At two, you'd sit
in the wicker laundry basket and watch TV

and play with matchbox cars, your eyes,
gray and clear. We lived in married-student
housing at Rutgers, those Quonset hut houses
with their small square backyards and the

morning glory vine I planted on the chicken
wire fence and the sandbox Grandma bought
for you. I'd watch you play with your Tonka
trucks for hours and hold you in my arms,

your head against my chest, your hair smelling
of Johnson's Baby Shampoo, and I'd read to you,
"One more book, Mom," you'd say. "Just one more."
That's the way it is with mothers and sons,

I swear I could close my eyes and imagine
you are still leaning against me while I read.
As you grew up, each year full of memories,
the boy I drove to track meetings, the way

you ran track every day, though every day
you threw up, other boys so accustomed to it
they didn't seem to notice. Strange how
the days and years spin faster and faster,

the images as you grow away from me
fewer but still clear. Clear until now, years
since you graduated from college and law
school, since your marriage, the birth of your

children, each year the gap between us growing
wider. This is the way it is between mothers
and sons, the mother unable to forget the boy
she held in her arms, the son wanting only

to be the man he's become – lover, husband, father –
and not any woman's son.

Everything We Don't
Want Them to Know

At eleven, my granddaughter looks like my daughter
did, that slender body, that thin face, the grace

with which she moves. When she visits, she sits
with my daughter; they have hot chocolate together

and talk. The way my granddaughter moves her hands,
the concentration with which she does everything,

knocks me back to the time when I sat with my daughter
at this table and we talked and I watched the grace

with which she moved her hands, the delicate way
she lifted the heavy hair back behind her ear.

My daughter is grown now, married
in a fairy-tale wedding, divorced, something inside

her broken, healing slowly. I look at my granddaughter
and I want to save her, as I was not able

to save my daughter. Nothing is that simple,
all our plans, carefully made, thrown into a cracked

pile by the way love betrays us.

At Eleven, My Granddaughter

For Caroline Paige Gillan

At eleven, my granddaughter loves to read,
her long, narrow body stretched out on the sofa,

a book in her hands. She reads for hours.
She takes her hand and gracefully lifts back

her thick, honey-blond hair, tucks it
behind her ear until it falls forward again.

She wears braces and serious glasses with metal frames.
She looks bright and concentrated as a flame.

She sings in a high sweet voice, the way
she sang along with the radio when she was very small,

and she'd ride strapped into her car seat and sing
everywhere they went. Even today, when she gets

into the car, she asks for a specific CD, and she drinks
in the music through all the pores of her skin.

She tells me she wants to be an artist,
and presents me with perfect pictures of animals

she's drawn freehand. Her life, mapped out,
a straight road from Hawkscrest Court in North Carolina

to another house just like her own. When she visits,
she says, "Oh, that's weird," or "You're weird,"

but I shout, "Who wants to be ordinary? How boring!"
and she watches me, as though I were a creature

from Mars, but I hope, years from now,
she'll remember what I've said. I wish her

a long velvet cape lined with scarlet satin,
a life she paints for herself, drawing it freehand,

the strokes of her brush loose and reckless, the picture
emerging, one large bright slash at a time.

My Daughter's Hands

My daughter tells me she has Grandma's hands,
referring to her father's mother who lived with us
for nine years after she had a heart attack. Later,
she went senile and imagined people were coming
out of the TV to get us. She called me over to her

ten times a day to warn me. My daughter's hands
are strong with pronounced veins, and she is convinced
they are her grandmother's. She remembers Grandma
fondly, the way she'd serve bowls of Spaghetti O's,
or count out the meatballs so each child would

have the same number, and how she'd put M&M's
in tin pie plates for them. She does not remember
the grandmother who was so angry finally that she
made a hole in the wall with her rocker,
but rather the woman who cooked bacon for her

and bought Sara Lee cakes. I tell my daughter
I think her hands are like mine, and my hands
come down to me from my mother, the same
square shape, the small fingers. If you looked
at our hands, you'd think we were delicate,

but we never give up, keep working until
we're too sick to move. Sometimes, when I look
at my hand, I imagine my mother reaching
for my hand, as she did so often
when she was still alive, imagine her

hand, brown from all the gardening she did,
tough and calloused, imagine that she is still
sitting with me when I see Dennis, slumped
and broken in his chair, when he says,
"I can't do this anymore," and I use her hands

to give him the courage to go on just as
my daughter uses her hands
to pat my back while I cry.

My Grandson and GI Joe

When he was three, I'd hold my grandson
and kiss his skin, tasting the sweetness that rose
off him. He'd laugh wildly as I made slurping
sounds, while I kissed the soft folds of skin

at his elbow, the bottoms of his wide feet.
My sweet-natured grandson is named Jackson
after a stern Civil War general, and he loves GI
Joe in all his incarnations – GI Joe Warrior and

GI Joe Scuba diver and GI Joe in jungle fatigues
and GI Joe tanks and armored cars, his room
populated with the murderous supplies of war.
My grandson, serious and self-contained, tells

stories to himself while he plays army; he
and his friends shoot tiny rifles, machine guns,
bazookas. They play at war. On TV the real
war is played out, the one where cities

are blasted out of existence, the one where
people die, the one where children are bereft
of arms and legs. My grandson and his friends
wear army fatigue jackets and pants. They chase

each other through the house and fall
elaborately, pretending to be wounded, and then
they rise again to lie flat on the floor and move
the GI Joe figures into action. My grandson

loves beautiful things, satin and velvet,
the smooth stones of my earrings and pendants,
the satin edge of a blanket. He is exuberant,
always thinks he will win the million

dollars promised behind the faces of bottle caps.
He collects tadpoles and holds them with careful
hands. That sweetness still rises off his skin
and emerges from the center of the boy

he has become. GI Joe is a story, a tale
he can create out of imagination and hope.
He doesn't know the exploding missiles on TV
kill people who can't get up, ever, to play again,

or wound soldiers, like those young men in
West Virginia in that article in the *New York Times,*
who went off to Iraq at nineteen, and six
months later returned to their blue-collar town

minus legs and arms, their bodies scarred, their
lives plagued by violent nightmares, so now
they say, "I'm afraid to sleep," and they spend
their nights in the flickering gray light instead,

afraid to close their eyes for fear
of who they'll see.

What We Pass On

For Jackson Stuart Gillan

My son is handsome, like my husband and grandson.
They look like cookie-cutter men, the three of them,

my husband obviously the oldest since his illness
left his face lined and drawn, and my son looks

exactly as his father looked at thirty-seven.
My grandson is a miniature version

of the two of them, but my son and grandson
walk the way I do on my flat feet, chunky

and turned out slightly, only they hit the ground
harder. My grandson emulates his father's walk,

his hands hooked in the pockets of his pants,
his shoulders swinging. Like his father, my son

never gives up. Like me, he needs to heal the world,
needs to be responsible for everyone.

Though my grandson is only seven, he reminds me
of my mother with her exuberant laugh,

her abundant energy, her loving heart, the parts
of all of us, even the ancestors I never met,

caught in my son and grandson. My grandson
trudges into the world on his wide feet, in him

I see my twin. I love the way he loves the feel
of my satin nightgown on his face, the way

he attacks his food with gusto, the way it makes him happy,
the way he looks in his little electric car that he piles

with leftover lumber from the construction site,
and he drives down the hill behind the house,

wearing his hard hat, dumps one load of wood,
goes back for another because he wants to build

a tree house. He drives up the street, stops
at Carina's house, picks her up and they ride off,

as though he had picked her up for a date.
How mixed up this genetic code that sends

my mother back to me in this boy
growing up in North Carolina

so far from any place
my mother had ever seen.

The Dead Are Not Silent

Long after their eyes turn opaque as frosted glass,
their faces still and empty,
long after the gravestones' chiseled faces,
long after the mourners' tears,
the dead return. First, they creep in,
and I imagine I hear a whisper, but when
I turn, there is no one there.

Sometimes it is a touch, light and soft
on my neck, or the lick of cold fingers
on my arm. Gradually, they grow bolder.
They come to my room at night.
I wake up to find them standing above me:

my mother, her face unlined, now a face
from which suffering has been erased.
Her eyes are as full of love as they were
when I could go to her every day.

Sometimes my father is there; his body
seems irrelevant and indistinct, not broken
as it was when he still lived.
I'd visit him every night after Mama died
so he wouldn't be lonely. We didn't

talk much. We'd watch his favorite
program, *Murder She Wrote*. I knew
he was happy to have me there,
as I am happy to have him visit me now.

Finally, my sister appears. She hasn't
even been gone a year. I can tell
she knows I miss her. The room

is crowded with the dead. They move in
and are a comforting presence.
Each day I mention them, remind myself

of something they did or said. I hear them
rustle as they move; their voices, silk scarves
that trail behind me.

What the Dead No Longer Need

The dead no longer need the world
with all its noise and clatter, the people
they loved on earth, their children
and grandchildren, old lovers,
whom they thought they couldn't
live without, the houses they polished
and paid for, the money they gave up
their lives to earn, the cars that made them
feel powerful, all the edges of people
and things no longer sharp and, gradually,
not there at all.

The dead no longer need us, or the world,
all irrelevant in the washed light of that other
place where they live now and where
we can't touch them.

We who are left behind still need them,
want to believe they still love us as they did:
my mother still my mother, my father
still my father, my sister still my sister.
If I reach out I can touch them. I say
their names a dozen times a day.
They do not hear. I imagine
they come back to comfort me, their ghosts
as real as pears in a bowl. But these
are the lies I tell myself.

The dead don't need us anymore.
In that other world they cannot hear us
call them. They have climbed
into a tower where they won't
let down their hair so we can climb it,
so filled we are with our need.

I Want to Celebrate

the small pleasures, the sweet taste of cappuccino
in my mouth, the slow melting of a chocolate square
on my tongue or sitting on a hotel bed
with my twelve-year-old granddaughter,
while we discuss the theme of the movie
we're watching, my granddaughter
with her serious face and her love of books,
the way she carries her book with her
wherever she goes, as I do, and the hug
she gives me when they leave that tells me
she does not want to let me go,
or that moment on the hotel balcony,
my nine-year-old grandson standing near
the railing, leaning his folded arms on it,
and looking out at the skyline of Washington
glowing against the darkening sky,
that moment when I realize
how alike we are, this grandson
whose breath catches when he looks at
the vista stretched out before us. "It makes
you feel so free," he says, both of us
smiling the same way.

The small pleasures, the aroma of basil and mint
at my mother's kitchen door, the heavy feel
of the purple figs from my father's fig tree
in my hand, the loamy smell of my mother's
garden, the glass figurines my daughter
bought me when she was a child,

the bouquet of tulips you gave me
because you knew I loved them, those moments
years ago when we'd walk through the woods together,
hands touching, the times you turn to me
and say, "I don't know what I'd do without you."

Couch Buddha

My daughter calls me Couch Buddha
because people always come to me
for advice and help and
because I give it even when
they don't ask, like my mother did,
because I pushed Paul into finishing
his book proposal,
because I pushed my hairdresser
into demanding respect from her husband,
because people call me on the phone
to ask me what to do,
and I sit on my sofa and tell them –
Couch Buddha who knows
exactly what everyone should do,
poor weak Buddha who eats
the troubles of the world
and answers riddles for everyone
but can't find the way out
for herself.

Acknowledgments

These poems have been previously published in the following journals and anthologies: "People Who Live Only in Photographs," "Little House on the Prairie," "Christmas Story," "I Am Thinking of the Dress," "Do You Know What It Is I Feel," published in *Louisiana Literature*; "There Was No Pleasing My Mother," "Breakfast at the IHOP," "Your Voice on the Phone Wobbles," "I Walk Through the Rooms of Memory," published in *Connecticut Review*; "Superman," "Selective Memory," published in *Prairie Schooner*; "Nighties," published in *New Letters*; "Trying to Get You to Love Me," "In the Movies No One Ever Ages," "On Thanksgiving This Year," published in *LIPS*; "My Father's Fig Tree Grew in Hawthorne," "Nothing Can Bring Back the Dead," "Couch Buddha," published in *VIA: Voices In Italian Americana*; "Spike-Heels," "At Eleven," "My Granddaughter," published in *Feminist Studies*; "What Did I Know About Love," published in *Edison Literary Review*; "I Want To Write a Poem to Celebrate," published in *Haight Ashbury Literary Journal*; "My Sister and Frank Sinatra," published in *Sinatra Anthology*; "My Father Always Drove," published in *Asphodel*; "The Photograph of Us on an Outing to Cold Spring," published in *Paddlefish*; "Driving Into Our New Lives," "What the Dead No Longer Need," published in *Pennsylvania English*.

By the Same Author

Printed in February 2007
at Gauvin Press, Gatineau, Québec